THE
LIFE
ROSARY

Powerful Prayers
to End Abortion
and Heal Hearts

MARY SAMBO

Caritas Press

THE LIFE ROSARY
Powerful Prayers to End Abortion and Heal Hearts

Mary Sambo

Editor: Sherry Boas
Copy Editor: Elsa Schiavone

For information regarding permission,
contact Sherry@LilyTrilogy.com

First Edition
10 9 8 7 6 5 4 3 2 1
ISBN 978-1-940209-34-0

Scripture passages from the New American Bible Revised Edition

This book was reviewed for doctrinal error by Fr. Don Kline, V.F., Pastor, St. Joan of Arc Roman Catholic Church, Phoenix, Ariz., Diocese of Phoenix.

For reorders, visit CaritasPress.org
(602) 920-2846

To my children in heaven—
Lee Anne,
David Paul,
and Amelia Rose

INTRODUCTION

"Surely I wait for the Lord; who bends down to me and hears my cry, draws me up from the pit of destruction, out of the muddy clay, sets my feet upon rock, steadies my steps, and puts a new song in my mouth, a hymn to our God." (Psalm 40:2-4)

I am one of the millions of women who have had an abortion. In 1971, I was sixteen years old and pregnant, two years before the historic Supreme Court decision on Roe v. Wade which legalized a woman's right to have an abortion. Without confiding in my parents, I flew from Michigan to New York City. New York was one of only two states inside the continent where abortion was legal upon request. [1] I lied about my identity and my age. I allowed a physician to end my child's life through a method called "vacuum aspiration." It was an excruciatingly painful procedure for me. It must have been torture for my unborn child. Moments later, I was lying in a bed in a room filled with dozens of other women who had just made the same decision.

Having an abortion is the biggest regret of my life. It's a decision I can never undo. It has rippled with negative effects in my life for years. I quickly learned it's not so easy to just eliminate a problem. Abortion actually brings on a host of new problems. I have dealt with the grief and guilt of the loss of my child for years. I went through decades of depression, suicide attempts, anger, sadness, anxiety, and promiscuity. I had

4

two miscarriages in the two years following my abortion.

But I am one of the fortunate ones. I have been able to stop this destructive cycle by asking God to forgive me. And I have been able to ask my child for forgiveness. I believe she is in heaven interceding for me daily.

Pope Saint John Paul II, in "The Gospel of Life," reaches out lovingly and compassionately to women who have had an abortion. While condemning abortion as "an unspeakable crime," he acknowledges that, "the decision to have an abortion is often tragic and painful for the mother." But there is hope.

"I would like to say a special word to women who have had an abortion. The Church is aware of the many factors which may have influenced your decision, and she does not doubt that in many cases it was a painful and even shattering decision. The wound in your heart may not yet have healed. Certainly what happened was and remains terribly wrong. But do not give in to discouragement and do not lose hope. With the friendly and expert help and advice of other people, and as a result of your own painful experience, you can become the most eloquent defenders of everyone's right to life." [2]

The purpose of this intercessory Rosary prayer book is to pray for people who have had an abortion and are still suffering from its deep wounds. My prayer is that they will seek repentance and find healing and peace through God. The book is also to pray for men and women today who are considering ending the life of their unborn child. My hope is that the petitions in this book before each Hail Mary of the Rosary will change their minds.

This book is meant to empower pro-life supporters in their battle to protect life and pray for those affected by abortion. There is so much we can do as God's soldiers. There is also a specific role where each one of us fits in and is called to act.

In *Champions of the Rosary: The History and Heroes of a Spiritual Weapon*, author Fr. Donald H. Calloway writes:

"The Rosary will make you an armed soldier, a sword-wielding knight on the battlefield of life."

So I pray that you arm yourself with the power of the Rosary and use this book as your sword in the battle.

HOW TO PRAY THE ROSARY WITH THIS INTERCESSORY PRAYER BOOK

(You can find the words to all the Rosary prayers in the Appendix at the end of this book.)

1. Begin by holding the crucifix and making the sign of the cross saying, "In the Name of the Father and of the Son and of the Holy Spirit."

2. Say the "Apostles Creed."

3. On the single bead just above the crucifix, say the "Our Father" prayer.

4. Next, you will see a cluster of three beads. The "Hail Mary" prayer is said on each of these beads. While saying the Hail Mary prayer three times, meditate on the three divine virtues of faith, hope, and charity.

5. On the single bead after these three beads, say the "Glory Be" and the "O My Jesus" prayers.

6. At this point, you are ready to announce the divine mystery of contemplation. For example, if it were a Monday, you would say, "The first Joyful Mystery—The Annunciation."

7. After announcing the mystery, read the meditation in this book for the mystery.

8. Then you are ready to say the "Our Father" prayer.

9. Now this will bring you to the first decade or set of 10 beads. One "Hail Mary" prayer is said on each of these beads. Before you pray each Hail Mary, say the short petition in this book that is written for a specific group of people affected by abortion.

10. After the tenth Hail Mary, you will come to another single bead. At this point, you say the "Glory Be" and the "O My Jesus" prayers. Some people also like to add the "Prayer for Priests" at the end of each decade. Stay on this bead to say the next "Our Father."

11. Continue this process for the next four decades of the Rosary. After saying five mysteries, you have said a "chaplet." Here is where you decide if you want to stop at one chaplet, or continue with another.

12. If you decide to say another chaplet, you simply announce the next mystery, such as the first of the Sorrowful Mysteries. Then continue with the next five mysteries you have chosen to meditate on.

13. When you are ready to end the chaplet, say the "Hail, Holy Queen" and "Closing Prayer." You may add any of the other prayers of the Rosary, such

as the "Memorare," "St. Michael Prayer," or other "Fatima Prayers," that you like to recite. Some people desire to include the "Litany of the Blessed Virgin Mary," and the "Prayer to St. Joseph" at the end of the Rosary.

14. The "Our Father" and "Hail Mary" prayers are added at the end of the Rosary for the Pope's intentions if you wish to gain a plenary indulgence.

15. End the Rosary with the sign of the cross saying, "In the name of the Father, and of the Son, and of the Holy Spirit, Amen."

A Note About the Format of Petitions:

In this book, I use the terms "couple" and "men and women." I realize it is the woman carrying the child, and in many cases, it is the woman alone making the decision to abort. Regardless, it is important to consider the man in the relationship. Even if he does not influence the decision, he should be included in prayer.

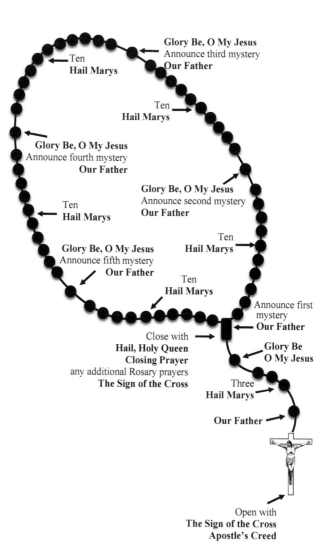

Glory Be, O My Jesus
Announce third mystery
Our Father

← Ten
Hail Marys

Ten →
Hail Marys

← **Glory Be, O My Jesus**
Announce fourth mystery
Our Father

Glory Be, O My Jesus
Announce second mystery
Our Father

← Ten
Hail Marys

Glory Be, O My Jesus
Announce fifth mystery
Our Father

Ten →
Hail Marys

Ten
Hail Marys

Announce first
mystery
Our Father

Close with →
Hail, Holy Queen
Closing Prayer
any additional Rosary prayers
The Sign of the Cross

Glory Be
O My Jesus

Three →
Hail Marys

Our Father →

Open with
The Sign of the Cross
Apostle's Creed

THE
JOYFUL
MYSTERIES

THE ANNUNCIATION

"Mary said, 'Behold, I am the handmaiden of The Lord. May it be done to me according to your word.'" (Luke 1:38)

Lord, reach out to the couple who have just learned of their unexpected pregnancy. Let them feel your presence. Calm their fears with confidence that you are near. Settle the anxiety in their minds with a gentle peace. Grant them the faith of Mary, who did not have all the answers either, when hearing she was to become your Mother.

Help the couple slow down in making their decision and ponder, as Mary did. Remove their doubts by reassuring them you will provide. Give them clarity amidst the voices of confusion. Send an angel to stand between them and the evil one who tries to fill their thoughts with abortion diguised as relief. Open their eyes to the lifetime of pain, suffering, and regret abortion brings.

Let them foresee the joys of being parents and raising a child. Give them the courage to follow in your Mother's footsteps, and answer "Yes" to the gift of life.

Our Father ...

Petitions:

1. May the mother and father facing an unexpected pregnancy not be afraid.
Hail Mary ...

2. May the mother and father of the unborn child ponder when hearing about their pregnancy, as Mary pondered, and realize that all life is sacred and sent from God.
Hail Mary ...

3. May the woman who has had an abortion, and the father of that child, know they can still find favor with God.
Hail Mary ...

4. May the relatives who have lost a family member through abortion know the Lord is with them.
Hail Mary ...

5. May the doctors and staff of abortion clinics, and all those who believe that abortion is a woman's right, know that all things came to be through God and without him nothing came to be.
Hail Mary ...

6. May the prayer warriors praying on the front lines at abortion clinics and in prayer groups see the glory of the Father's only Son, full of grace and truth.
Hail Mary ...

7. May pregnancy help center staff and sidewalk counselors testify to the light; the true light which enlightens everyone.
Hail Mary ...

8. May the priests ministering to those experiencing an unexpected pregnancy and those affected by an abortion make a connection with the greatly troubled, and help them draw closer to God.
Hail Mary ...

9. May the Church, whose faithful have the opportunity to minister to those affected by unexpected pregnancy and abortion, be the light that shines in the darkness.
Hail Mary ...

10. May those involved in pro-life movements and abortion recovery be continually blessed for the work they do, and their passion be renewed daily, knowing nothing will be impossible for God.
Hail Mary ...
Glory Be ...

THE VISITATION

"During those days Mary set out and traveled to the hill country in haste to a town of Judah, where she entered the house of Zachariah and greeted Elizabeth. When Elizabeth heard Mary's greeting, the infant leaped in her womb, and Elizabeth, filled with the Holy Spirit, cried out in a loud voice and said, 'Most blessed are you among women, and blessed is the fruit of your womb.'" (Luke 1:39-42)

Lord, just as Mary visited Elizabeth in haste, quickly send the couple of an unexpected pregnancy the perfect visitor. Let it be someone who the couple feels comfortable talking to about their situation. And let it be someone who will be excited about the life conceived. Draw the couple to confide in him or her. Bind the devil from confounding the couple with fears of talking about their pregnancy. Silence any dissenting voices among parents, friends and relatives.

Prepare the perfect confidant to withhold judgement and give sound advice and loving support. Give him or her the words to reach the deepest part of the couple's hearts where decisions are made. Help this couple recognize that their child is a miracle from you and worthy of life.

Our Father ...

Petitions:

1. May the mother and father facing an unexpected pregnancy seek pro-life counseling in haste before thoughts of abortion creep in.
Hail Mary ...

2. May the mother and father of the unborn child understand how blessed is the fruit of the womb.
Hail Mary ...

3. May the woman who has had an abortion, and the father of that child, know God's mercy is from age to age.
Hail Mary ...

4. May the relatives who have lost a family member through abortion allow their spirits to rejoice in God their savior.
Hail Mary ...

5. May the arrogance be dispersed in the minds and hearts of doctors and staff of abortion clinics, and all those who believe that abortion is a woman's right, so they may hear the pro-life message.
Hail Mary ...

6. May the prayer warriors praying on the front lines at abortion clinics and in prayer groups be filled with the Holy Spirit and know they are blessed because they believe that the Word of the Lord will be fulfilled.
Hail Mary ...

7. May the greetings of pregnancy help center staff and sidewalk counselors reach the ears of pregnant couples, and may the Holy Spirit draw them in to listen.
Hail Mary ...

8. May the priests ministering to those experiencing an unexpected pregnancy and those affected by an abortion proclaim the greatness of the Lord, and his desire to lift them up.
Hail Mary ...

9. May the Church, whose faithful have the opportunity to minister to those affected by unexpected pregnancy and abortion, remember God's mercy towards all his people.
Hail Mary ...

10. May those involved in pro-life movements and abortion recovery have confidence that the Lord is their help, and that he will continue to do great things for them.
Hail Mary ...
Glory Be ...

THE BIRTH OF CHRIST

"While they were there, the time came for her to have her child and she gave birth to her firstborn son. She wrapped him in swaddling clothes and laid him in a manger because there was no room for them in the inn." (Luke 2:6-7)

Heavenly Father, Mary's "Yes" led to the birth of your Son, Our Redeemer. In Mary's heart, mind, and soul, there was only one choice for her — to follow your will. Open the eyes of the couple with an unexpected pregnancy so they may see your will for them to give birth to their child. Prevent Satan from tempting the couple to end the child's life prematurely through abortion. Exhaust them with thoughts of the grief that would follow from the loss of their baby. Melt away the hardness of heart of the man or woman who claim there will be no regret from abortion.

Show the couple the joys of giving birth. Give them visions of Mary kissing your face as a newborn. Assure them that you will miraculously provide for their needs.

Our Father ...

Petitions:

1. May the mother and father facing an unexpected pregnancy be aided by the comfort of the Lord.
Hail Mary ...

2. May the mother and father of the unborn child receive the pregnancy as news of great joy.
Hail Mary ...

3. May the woman who has had an abortion, and the father of that child, know God can bring them peace.
Hail Mary ...

4. May the relatives who have lost a family member through abortion know God is with them.
Hail Mary ...

5. May the hearts of doctors and staff of abortion clinics, and all those who believe that abortion is a woman's right, be softened enough to acknowledge that the infant in the manger is a sign of the miracle of life and its creator.
Hail Mary ...

6. May the prayer warriors praying on the front lines at abortion clinics and in prayer groups know that angels surround them, singing "Glory to God in the highest heaven."
Hail Mary ...

7. May pregnancy help center staff and sidewalk counselors convince couples there is no place where God is not present, and therefore, no reason to lose hope or joy.
Hail Mary ...

8. May the priests ministering to those experiencing an unexpected pregnancy and those affected by an abortion say, "Peace on those on whom his favor rests."
Hail Mary ...

9. May the Church, whose faithful have the opportunity to minister to those affected by unexpected pregnancy and abortion, make room in their hearts for the troubled and hurting.
Hail Mary ...

10. May those involved in pro-life movements and abortion recovery communicate the message of salvation in all they do, and may all who hear it be amazed.
Hail Mary ...
Glory Be ...

THE PRESENTATION

"When the days were completed for their purification according to the law of Moses, they took him up to Jerusalem to present him to the Lord." (Luke 2:22)

Lord, at the presentation in the temple, Simeon and Anna talk to Joseph and Mary about Jesus' destiny. Simeon and Anna confirm what Joseph and Mary already know. Grant courage to the couple who fears the uncertain future of their unborn child. Reveal to these parents all the wonderful possibilities for the life of the baby they will bring into the world.

Jesus, protect and grant graces to every child born. Move the hearts of parents to serve you and raise their child to believe in you. Strengthen the couple so they may accept the responsibility of training their child in the practice of the Catholic faith, beginning with baptizing their baby. And may the couple who doesn't know your Church, or understand its sacraments, be lead to the faith.

Our Father ...

Petitions:

1. May the mother and father facing an unexpected pregnancy be obedient to God by saying, "Yes," to life.
Hail Mary ...

2. May the mother and father of the unborn child consecrate their child to the service of the Lord.
Hail Mary ...

3. May the woman who has had an abortion, and the father of that child, see the salvation the Lord has offered them.
Hail Mary ...

4. May the relatives who have lost a family member through abortion know that Jesus' birth is their consolation.
Hail Mary ...

5. May the Holy Spirit reveal to the doctors and staff of abortion clinics, and all those who believe that abortion is a woman's right, the evil that dwells in their hearts.
Hail Mary ...

6. May the prayer warriors praying on the front lines at abortion clinics and in prayer groups have the faith of Simeon and Anna.
Hail Mary ...

7. May pregnancy help center staff and sidewalk counselors help others to see your salvation.
Hail Mary ...

8. May the priests ministering to those experiencing an unexpected pregnancy and those affected by an abortion know the promises of the Lord.
Hail Mary ...

9. May the Church, whose faithful have the opportunity to minister to those affected by unexpected pregnancy and abortion, show Christ's light to all who seek it.
Hail Mary ...

10. May those involved in pro-life movements and abortion recovery worship night and day with fasting and prayer, so they may receive your graces.
Hail Mary ...
Glory Be ...

FINDING JESUS IN THE TEMPLE

"When his parents saw him, they were astonished, and his mother said to him, 'Son, why have you done this to us? Your father and I have been looking for you with great anxiety.'" (Luke 2:48)

Blessed Virgin Mary, Mother of God, who knows the great anxiety over the loss of a child, touch the hearts of a couple with an unexpected pregnancy and let them feel the gravity of the loss of a child through abortion. Let them feel the emptiness that will follow. Help their minds comprehend the regret of not being able to turn back time and make a different choice.

For those couples who have already lost their child through abortion, dear Mother, guide them to the temple of their soul—the place created for Jesus alone. Convince them there is no solace anywhere else. Intercede for them to your Son, to grant them consolation and grace.

Our Father ...

Petitions:

1. May Mary, who knows the great anxiety over a lost child, reveal to the mother and father facing an unexpected pregnancy, the loss and grief they will feel if they end their child's life.
Hail Mary ...

2. May the mother and father of the unborn child look forward to the blessing of taking their child in their arms.
Hail Mary ...

3. May the woman who has had an abortion, and the father of that child, find Jesus in the temple of their heart, and realize he has been there all along.
Hail Mary ...

4. May the relatives who have lost a family member through abortion keep the Word of the Lord in their heart.
Hail Mary ...

5. May the doctors and staff of abortion clinics, and all those who believe that abortion is a woman's right, ask questions that will lead them to the knowledge of the sacredness of life.
Hail Mary ...

6. May the prayer warriors praying on the front lines at abortion clinics and in prayer groups continue to be about their Heavenly Father's business.
Hail Mary ...

7. May pregnancy help center staff and sidewalk counselors impact the couples they contact with their understanding and answers.
Hail Mary ...

8. May the priests help those experiencing an unexpected pregnancy and those affected by an abortion find the love of the Lord.
Hail Mary ...

9. May the Church, whose faithful have the opportunity to minister to those affected by an unexpected pregnancy and abortion, welcome all into the Father's house.
Hail Mary ...

10. May those involved in pro-life movements and abortion recovery advance in wisdom and favor before God and man.
Hail Mary ...
Glory Be ...

THE
LUMINOUS
MYSTERIES

THE BAPTISM OF THE LORD

"After all the people had been baptized and Jesus also had been baptized and was praying, heaven was opened and the Holy Spirit descended upon him in bodily form like a dove. And a voice came from heaven, 'You are my beloved Son; with you I am well pleased.'" (Luke 3:21-22)

Lord, thank you for the indelible spiritual mark I received by grace in baptism. By this sacrament, I am adopted as your child and consecrated to live a life of charity.

Help me demonstrate that charity through the Spiritual Works of Mercy. Help me instruct the ignorant through non-confrontational conversations about being pro-life. Give me the words and sincerity to counsel those who are considering abortion, or those who doubt your forgiveness.

Remind me to bear wrongs patiently if I am taunted, honked at, or yelled at, while standing up for life. Help me to forgive those offenses. Make me receptive to the afflicted, wherever I meet them, so I can give them comfort. Never let me forget to pray for the living and the dead.

Our Father ...

Petitions:

1. May the Lord send his messenger to the mother and father facing an unexpected pregnancy before they reach an abortion clinic.
Hail Mary ...

2. May the Lord lead the mother and father of the unborn child straight to him.
Hail Mary ...

3. May the woman who has had an abortion, and the father of that child, behold the Lamb of God who takes away the sins of the world.
Hail Mary ...

4. May the Spirit of the Lord descend on the relatives who have lost a family member through abortion and console their sorrows.
Hail Mary ...

5. May the Lord give light to those who live in darkness, like the doctors and staff of abortion clinics, and all those who believe that abortion is a woman's right.
Hail Mary ...

6. May the heavens open up when the prayer warriors pray on the front lines at abortion clinics and in prayer groups.
Hail Mary ...

7. May pregnancy help center staff and sidewalk counselors prepare the way for those who need them.
Hail Mary ...

8. May the priests ministering to those experiencing an unexpected pregnancy and those affected by an abortion remember the vows of their baptism.
Hail Mary ...

9. May the Lord guide the feet of those in the Church to those most in need of hearing the message of life.
Hail Mary ...

10. May those involved in pro-life movements and abortion recovery be our voice crying out in the desert.
Hail Mary ...
Glory Be ...

THE WEDDING OF CANA

"Now there were six stone water jars there for Jewish ceremonial washings, each holding twenty to thirty gallons. Jesus told them, 'Fill the jars with water.' So they filled them to the brim." (John 2:6-7)

Jesus, make me obedient like the servants at the wedding who followed your instructions to fill the jars with water. By their obedience, you blessed the guests with the best wine.

Lord, through this miracle, I see the connection between my obedience and your desire to bestow on me bountiful graces. You have commanded me not to kill. Your word says human beings have been made in the image of God, and you will demand an accounting for the loss of human life.

Lord, I consecrate my life to you and pledge my obedience to your commandments. Give me the grace to do all I can to preserve the lives of the unborn.

Our Father ...

Petitions:

1. May the mother and father facing an unexpected pregnancy know that their child is part of God's creation.
Hail Mary ...

2. May the mother and father of the unborn child understand God's sovereignty.
Hail Mary ...

3. May the woman who has had an abortion, and the father of that child, seek Mary, the Mother of God, knowing that Jesus listens to her requests.
Hail Mary ...

4. May the relatives who have lost a family member through abortion trust in the Lord who changes water into wine.
Hail Mary ...

5. May the commandment, "You shall not kill" continually interrupt the thoughts of the doctors and staff of abortion clinics, and all those who believe that abortion is a woman's right.
Hail Mary ...

6. May the prayer warriors praying on the front lines at abortion clinics and in prayer groups have the faith of Mary, who acted on her belief in Jesus, and set a miracle into action.
Hail Mary ...

7. May pregnancy help center staff and sidewalk counselors know that, if they have needs, they can go to Mary, the Mother of God, who said to Jesus, "They have no wine."
Hail Mary ...

8. May the priests ministering to those experiencing an unexpected pregnancy and those affected by an abortion reveal God's glory to those they counsel.
Hail Mary ...

9. May the Church, whose faithful have the opportunity to minister to those affected by unexpected pregnancy and abortion, share the story of the Wedding at Cana so that others may believe in him.
Hail Mary ...

10. May those involved in pro-life movements and abortion recovery help us follow Mary's instruction to "Do whatever he tells you."
Hail Mary ...
Glory Be ...

THE PROCLAMATION OF THE KINGDOM

"After John had been arrested, Jesus came to Galilee proclaiming the gospel of God: 'This is the time of fulfillment. The kingdom of God is at hand. Repent, and believe in the gospel.'" (Mark 1:14-15)

Jesus, when you went about proclaiming the kingdom of God, you talked many times about the importance of children. You ache for children to come to you. And you want us all to become like little children to enter your kingdom.

It is clear to me, Lord, that children hold a special place in your heart. It follows, then, that you would want me to do everything I can to protect their lives. Help me to become like a child in thought and deed for the sake of my salvation. Open the doors to opportunities to protect the unborn.

Our Father ...

Petitions:

1. May the mother and father facing an unexpected pregnancy know that after a woman gives birth to her child, she no longer remembers the pain because of the joy that child brings into the world.
Hail Mary ...

2. May the mother and father of the unborn child know that children are a heritage from the Lord, and the fruit of the womb is a gift.
Hail Mary ...

3. May the woman who regrets her abortion, and turns to Jesus for forgiveness, know that God has turned her mourning into dancing and clothed her with gladness.
Hail Mary ...

4. May the relatives who have lost a family member through abortion not despair, but be filled with hope.
Hail Mary ...

5. May the doctors and staff of abortion clinics, and all those who believe that abortion is a woman's right, hear Jesus' proclamation, "Repent, for the kingdom of heaven has come near."
Hail Mary ...

6. May the prayer warriors praying on the front lines at abortion clinics and in prayer groups be like children shouting in the temple courts, "Hosanna to the Son of David."
Hail Mary ...

7. May pregnancy help center staff and sidewalk counselors convince couples that God formed their inmost beings; He knit them in their mothers' wombs, and they are wonderfully made.
Hail Mary ...

8. May the priests ministering to those experiencing an unexpected pregnancy and those affected by an abortion remind them that God knew them before they were born.
Hail Mary ...

9. May the Church, whose faithful have the opportunity to minister to those affected by unexpected pregnancy and abortion, continue to be the light of the world.
Hail Mary ...

10. May those involved in pro-life movements and abortion recovery remind us that the unborn are children God has graciously given us.
Hail Mary ...
Glory Be ...

THE TRANSFIGURATION

"… he took Peter, John and James and went up the mountain to pray. While he was praying his face changed in appearance and his clothing became dazzling white. … a cloud came and cast a shadow over them, and they became frightened when they entered the cloud. Then from the cloud came a voice that said, 'This is my chosen Son; listen to him.'" (Luke 9:28-29, 34-35)

Lord, you were praying before your transfiguration. Help my prayers create in me a transfiguration of the heart. Make communing with you in prayer my heart's desire. Prayer will bring me closer to you. And the closer I get to you, the more I will become like you. Then your light will shine through me, and my countenance will be changed to yours.

I long for this change so that I may be a light to the world. I want people to see you in me. I want to be ready to encounter anyone, on any day, and to be ready with my testimony so that others might believe in you.

Jesus, help me to be fervent and dedicated in prayer. Help me reflect your goodness to others so they believe my testimony of life.

Our Father ...

Petitions:

1. May the uncertainty in the hearts of the mother and father facing an unexpected pregnancy be transfigured into the unselfishness of Christ.
Hail Mary ...

2. May the hearts of the mother and father of the unborn child be changed by the tenderness of Jesus.
Hail Mary ...

3. May the woman who has had an abortion, and the father of that child, feel Jesus' touch and hear him say, "Rise and do not be afraid."
Hail Mary ...

4. May the relatives who have lost a family member through abortion raise their eyes and see no one but Jesus alone.
Hail Mary ...

5. May the evil of abortion sicken the doctors and staff of abortion clinics, and all those who believe that abortion is a woman's right.
Hail Mary ...

6. May the radiance caught from heaven shine through the prayer warriors praying on the front lines at abortion clinics and in prayer groups.
Hail Mary ...

7. May the Christ-like spirit of the pregnancy help center staff and sidewalk counselors reveal itself in undimmed beauty.
Hail Mary ...

8. May the priests ministering to those experiencing an unexpected pregnancy and those affected by an abortion reflect God in all they do.
Hail Mary ...

9. May Christ's reflection be visible in the faces and lives of the Church, whose faithful have the opportunity to minister to those affected by unexpected pregnancy and abortion.
Hail Mary ...

10. May those involved in pro-life movements and abortion recovery help us hear God's voice that said, "This is my beloved Son, with whom I am well pleased; listen to him."
Hail Mary ...
Glory Be ...

THE INSTITUTION OF THE EUCHARIST

"Then he took the bread, said the blessing, broke it, and gave it to them, saying, 'This is my body which will be given for you; do this in memory of me.' And likewise the cup after they had eaten, saying, 'This cup is the new covenant in my blood, which will be shed for you.'" (Luke 22:19-20)

Thank you, Lord, for your sacrifice of love. You allowed your precious body to be broken and your blood shed so that we might have life, and have it more abundantly. Help pregnant couples make that same sacrifice of themselves and their needs for the sake of their child.

Lord, you said, "This is my body which will be given for you." Let us pray that pregnant couples give their body unselfishly for the needs of their child.

Jesus, we have faith that the Eucharist is your body and blood; let us also see that the newly formed embryo is a complete person.

Lord, you gave your life with love and courage. Help me to defend life with that same love and courage. By your cross, you gave us victory over death; give us also victory over abortion.

Let the Eucharist be the stregthening food I need in the defense for life.

Our Father ...

Petitions:

1.May the mother and father facing an unexpected pregnancy celebrate life and accept the child they have created.
Hail Mary ...

2. May the mother and father of the unborn child make the sacrifice of love and save their child's life.
Hail Mary ...

3. May the woman who has had an abortion, and the father of that child, know the blood of the Lamb was poured out for the forgiveness of sins.
Hail Mary ...

4. May the relatives who have lost a family member through abortion know God will raise us up on the last day.
Hail Mary ...

5. May the doctors and staff of abortion clinics, and all those who believe that abortion is a woman's right, know that the body and blood of Jesus was broken for the body and blood of the unborn.
Hail Mary ...

6. May the prayer warriors praying on the front lines at abortion clinics and in prayer groups say, "We believe, and have come to know, you are the Holy One of God."
Hail Mary ...

7. May pregnancy help center staff and sidewalk counselors show the fruits of your redemption to others.
Hail Mary ...

8. May the priests ministering to those experiencing an unexpected pregnancy, and those affected by an abortion, reveal to them the high priest and mediator of the new and eternal covenant.
Hail Mary ...

9. May the Church, whose faithful have the opportunity to minister to those affected by unexpected pregnancy and abortion, be ready to humbly wash the feet of others, as Jesus did.
Hail Mary ...

10. May those involved in pro-life movements and abortion recovery give us the message of eternal life.
Hail Mary ...
Glory Be ...

THE
SORROWFUL
MYSTERIES

THE AGONY IN THE GARDEN

"He took along Peter and the two sons of Zebedee, and began to feel sorrow and distress. Then he said to them, 'My soul is sorrowful even unto death.'" (Mathew 26:37-38)

Lord, give grace to the couple who will struggle with the decision of how to handle an unexpected pregnancy. Grant them the strength and courage to choose life and face the responsibilities of parenthood in the same way you accepted the cross in the Garden of Gethsemane.

I pray especially for the man or woman who does not know you. Show yourself to that person in a way that will change his or her life. Help that man or woman build a relationship with you as Lord and Savior.

Lord, I pray also for the man or woman who is a believer. Even those who know you can be tempted with the thought of abortion as a solution to an unexpected pregnancy. Soften that person's heart to be receptive to the call for life.

Lord, help the couple who has already taken the life of their child through abortion. They may be in great pain and despair. You were sorrowful even unto death in the garden, so you understand that depth of grief. Protect them from oppressive thoughts of depression or suicide. Flood their minds with thoughts of your love and endless tender mercies.

Our Father ...

Petitions:

1. May the mother and father facing an unexpected pregnancy know the sorrow that will come over them if they abort their child.
Hail Mary ...

2. May the mother and father of the unborn child pray as Jesus did in the Garden of Gethsemane, "Not as I will, but as you will."
Hail Mary ...

3. May the Lord, who knows great sorrow, protect the woman who has had an abortion, and the father of that child, from depression and suicide.
Hail Mary ...

4. May an angel from heaven strengthen and comfort the relatives who have lost a family member through abortion.
Hail Mary ...

5. May the doctors and staff of abortion clinics, and all those who believe that abortion is a woman's right, be awakened from their sleep and repent of their sins.
Hail Mary ...

6. May the prayer warriors praying on the front lines at abortion clinics and in prayer groups, pray fervently, as Jesus did in the garden, when his sweat became like drops of blood falling to the ground.
Hail Mary ...

7. May pregnancy help center staff and sidewalk counselors remain awake in the Garden with Jesus and keep watch with him.
Hail Mary ...

8. May the priests calm the anxiety, confusion and despair experienced by those with an unexpected pregnancy and those affected by an abortion, and help them to trust in God saying, "Abba, Father, all things are possible for you.".
Hail Mary ...

9. May the Church, whose faithful have the opportunity to minister to those affected by unexpected pregnancy and abortion, remain alert to serve others.
Hail Mary ...

10. May those involved in pro-life movements and abortion recovery strengthen our spirits where the flesh is weak, so we are willing to stand up for the right to life.
Hail Mary ...
Glory Be ...

THE SCOURGING AT THE PILLAR

"Pilate addressed them a third time, 'What evil has this man done? I found him guilty of no capital crime. Therefore I shall have him flogged and then release him.' With loud shouts, however, they persisted in calling for his crucifixion, and their voices prevailed." (Luke 23:22-23)

Jesus, you know what it is like to be mocked and ridiculed. Send your compassionate graces to pro-life supporters who are taunted by the voices of the pro-choice crowd. Give pro-life supporters the strength to stand strong amidst the voices for choice, and remain firm and faithful to their commitment to life. Grant pro-life supporters wisdom for talking to individuals who believe in the right to choose death for the unborn.

Lord, open the eyes of pregnant couples so they may see through the lies of the pro-choice movement. Reveal the dishonesty of claims that abortion is safe and that the right to choose death for another is a fundamental freedom. Let couples learn of the long-lasting side effects they may suffer when they choose to abort their child.

God, please comfort the couple who has already aborted a child. Cover their pain, sorrow and confusion with your gracious mercy. Give them hope. Send the couple someone who will testify to your boundless forgiveness.

Our Father ...

Petitions:

1. May the mother and father facing an unexpected pregnancy hear the voices for life over the voices for choice in the stirred-up crowd.
Hail Mary ...

2. May the mother and father of the unborn child stand strong against anyone questioning their choice for life.
Hail Mary ...

3. May the woman who has had an abortion, and the father of that child, find comfort in Christ's promise of forgiveness.
Hail Mary ...

4. May the relatives who have lost a family member through abortion listen to God's voice and begin to understand the anguish their loved one went through in making the decision to abort.
Hail Mary ...

5. May the doctors and staff of abortion clinics, and all those who believe that abortion is a woman's right, know the pain that Christ bore and the sufferings he endured for the children they put to death and their families.
Hail Mary ...

6. May the prayer warriors praying on the front lines at abortion clinics and in prayer groups plead for forgiveness for the sins of all mankind, especially for sins of the flesh.
Hail Mary ...

7. May the pro-life voices of the pregnancy help center staff and sidewalk counselors prevail over the cries for choice.
Hail Mary ...

8. May the priests ministering to those experiencing an unexpected pregnancy and those affected by an abortion, help couples understand that, by the wounds of Christ, we are healed.
Hail Mary ...

9. May the Church, whose faithful have the opportunity to minister to those affected by an unexpected pregnancy and abortion, not be indifferent towards these hurting souls, as Pilate was to Jesus.
Hail Mary ...

10. May those involved in pro-life movements and abortion recovery bear witness to the truth.
Hail Mary ...
Glory Be ...

THE CROWNING WITH THORNS

"Weaving a crown out of thorns, they placed it on his head, and a reed in his right hand. And kneeling before him, they mocked him, saying, 'Hail, King of the Jews!' They spat upon him and took the reed and kept striking him on the head."
(Matthew 27:29-30)

Oh, King of Kings, who was crowned with thorns, spat on, humiliated, and rejected, help the couple who would treat their unborn child in the same way. Lead the couple to accept, love, honor and appreciate the gift of life.

Lord, you faced the injustice of the crowd; you know the injustice of the children being murdered daily as they are torn from their mothers' wombs. I pray that all people will learn to respect life.

Dear Jesus, you know what it is like to be tortured. You understand the mental, physical and spiritual anguish in many couples who have put their child to death by abortion. I pray for the healing of their heart, mind, and spirit.

Our Father ...

Petitions:

1. May the mother and father facing an unexpected pregnancy understand the brutality of abortion.
Hail Mary ...

2. May the mother and father of the unborn child ask themselves, "What harm has the child done?" instead of sending the child to death.
Hail Mary ...

3. May the woman who has had an abortion, and the father of that child, know the Righteous One will make many righteous.
Hail Mary ...

4. May the relatives who have lost a family member through abortion meditate on how Christ felt when he was crowned with thorns so they may understand the pain and degradation often felt by post-abortive couples.
Hail Mary ...

5. May the doctors and staff of abortion clinics, and all those who believe that abortion is a woman's right, know that they cannot simply wash their hands of the sin of abortion, nor are they innocent of the blood of children.
Hail Mary ...

6. May the prayer warriors praying on the front lines at abortion clinics and in prayer groups endure any ignorance, taunting, cruelty or mocking from the pro-choice crowd.
Hail Mary ...

7. May pregnancy help center staff and sidewalk counselors help pregnant couples remove themselves from the shouting crowd and exercise their own conscience to discern between good and evil.
Hail Mary ...

8. May the priests ministering to those experiencing an unexpected pregnancy and those affected by an abortion explain that Jesus endured unspeakable pain for us.
Hail Mary ...

9. May the Church, whose faithful have the opportunity to minister to those affected by unexpected pregnancy and abortion, embrace these couples with understanding of their suffering and pain.
Hail Mary ...

10. May those involved in pro-life movements and abortion recovery help us all understand emotional and psychological effects of abortion.
Hail Mary ...
Glory Be ...

THE CARRYING OF THE CROSS

"Then he handed him over to them to be crucified. So they took Jesus, and carrying the cross himself, he went out to what is called the Place of the Skull, in Hebrew, Golgotha." (John 19:16-17)

Lord, the couple with an unexpected pregnancy may feel as though giving birth to their child is too much for them to bear. Just as your cross was heavy, the responsibility of raising a child may feel like a heavy weight, pressing against them, overwhelming. And just as you walked alone, their path may seem lonely – a hard road, with pitfalls that will cause them to stumble. Send the mother and father someone to help carry their burden, like Simon of Cyrene bore the cross for you. Encourage them to accept their vocation as parents.

Jesus, the road for the couple who has aborted their child is a weary one too. Walk along side them and make your presence known. Lead them to your path of forgiveness and healing. Let them know they are not alone.

Our Father ...

Petitions:

1. May the mother and father facing an unexpected pregnancy know they do not have to carry their cross alone, for the yoke of God is easy and his burden is light.
Hail Mary ...

2. May the mother and father of the unborn child see their pregnancy as a gift rather than a cross to bear.
Hail Mary ...

3. May the woman who has had an abortion, and the father of that child, meet Mary, the Mother of God, who knows the untold anguish in their hearts.
Hail Mary ...

4. May the relatives who have lost a family member through abortion find rest for their souls.
Hail Mary ...

5. May the doctors and staff of abortion clinics, and all those who believe that abortion is a woman's right, weep for themselves and for the children whose life they have ended.
Hail Mary ...

6. May the prayer warriors praying on the front lines at abortion clinics and in prayer groups mourn and lament for those who are hurting.
Hail Mary ...

7. May pregnancy crisis center staff and sidewalk counselors be like Simon of Cyrene and help others carry their cross.
Hail Mary ...

8. May the priests ministering to those experiencing an unexpected pregnancy and those affected by an abortion show those they counsel how to take up their cross daily and follow Jesus.
Hail Mary ...

9. May the Church, whose faithful have the opportunity to minister to those affected by unexpected pregnancy and abortion, have compassion for those who have chosen abortion, regardless of how many times they have stumbled.
Hail Mary ...

10. May those involved in pro-life movements and abortion recovery reflect the the light of God's countenance in all they say and do.
Hail Mary ...
Glory Be ...

THE CRUCIFIXTION

"It was now about noon and darkness came over the whole land until three in the afternoon because of an eclipse of the sun. Then the veil of the temple was torn down the middle. Jesus cried out in a loud voice, 'Father, into your hands I commend my spirit;' and when he had said this he breathed his last." (Luke 23:44-46)

Savior, you experienced the worst form of death as payment for our sins. Your flesh was torn as you hung with your hands and feet nailed against the hard wood of the cross. Your side was pierced, and blood and water flowed. I pray for the innocent baby whose tiny body is pierced by the abortionist until blood and water flows and torn from his or her mother's womb. I pray that pregnant couples see abortion as the abhorrent sin that it is.

Despite the horror of abortion, we remember your words while hanging from the cross, "Father, forgive them for they know not what they do." With compassion for us, you pleaded to the Father on our behalf. I pray that any couple who has gone through an abortion knows they can receive forgiveness through your saving grace.

Our Father ...

Petitions:

1. May the mother and father facing an unexpected pregnancy not succumb to the brutality and ignorance of abortion.
Hail Mary ...

2. May the mother and father of the unborn child, though they feel scared and confused, choose to love their child as God so loved the world.
Hail Mary ...

3. May the woman who has had an abortion, and the father of that child, know that Jesus poured out his blood for the forgiveness of sins.
Hail Mary ...

4. May the relatives who have lost a family member through abortion know the child's spirit has been commended into the hands of the Father.
Hail Mary ...

5. May the doctors and staff of abortion clinics, and all those who believe that abortion is a woman's right, understand that if they refuse God's love, then they are condemned, not by God, but by their own thoughts and deeds.[3]
Hail Mary ...

6. May the prayer warriors praying on the front lines at abortion clinics and in prayer groups pray, "Father, forgive them, they know not what they do."
Hail Mary ...

7. May pregnancy help center staff and sidewalk counselors convince pregnant couples they have not been abandoned.
Hail Mary ...

8. May the priests ministering to those experiencing an unexpected pregnancy and those affected by an abortion declare that there is no condemnation for those who are in Christ Jesus.
Hail Mary ...

9. May the Church, whose faithful have the opportunity to minister to those affected by unexpected pregnancy and abortion, hold out their hands in love the way Jesus stretched out his arms to save us.
Hail Mary ...

10. May those involved in pro-life movements and abortion recovery reveal to us the Divine Mercy of Jesus' sacrifice on the cross.
Hail Mary ...
Glory Be ...

THE
GLORIOUS
MYSTERIES

THE RESSURECTION

"Then the angel said to the women in reply, 'Do not be afraid! I know that you are seeking Jesus the crucified. He is not here, for he has been raised just as he said.'" (Matthew 28:5-6)

Dear Father in heaven, thank you for the gift of your Son, Jesus. His rising from the dead changed mankind for eternity. His resurrection gave us victory over sin, death, and every part of our human nature that wants to turn away from you.

Lord, the innocents who die as a result of abortion did not have the opportunity to know you. They were not baptized. They did not know the way of salvation. But Lord, you said, "Let the children come to me, do not hinder them." This gives me faith that these precious little ones are with you in heaven. I trust that you show these souls the same mercy and love that you show the Church. I have faith that they are enjoying the same promise of salvation shared by the family of God.

Our Father ...

Petitions:

1. May the power of Jesus' resurrection give the mother and father who are facing an unexpected pregnancy victory over everything that crushes life.
Hail Mary ...

2. May the mother and father of the unborn child hear Jesus say, "Do not be afraid."
Hail Mary ...

3. May the woman who has had an abortion, and the father of that child, be comforted by Jesus' words, "I will see you again, and your hearts will rejoice, and no one will take your joy away from you."
Hail Mary ...

4. May the relatives who have lost a family member through abortion remember Jesus' words, "Your grief will become joy."
Hail Mary ...

5. May the doctors and staff of abortion clinics, and all those who believe that abortion is a woman's right, be reminded of the power of God, who forever holds the keys of eternal life.
Hail Mary ...

6. May the prayer warriors praying on the front lines at abortion clinics and in prayer groups know that, through the Holy Spirit, God has clothed them with power from on high.
Hail Mary ...

7. May pregnancy help center staff and sidewalk counselors calm the troubled minds and answer the questions in the hearts of those they encounter.
Hail Mary ...

8. May the hearts of those experiencing an unexpected pregnancy and those affected by an abortion burn with readiness to hear the Lord as priests minister to their needs.
Hail Mary ...

9. May the Church, whose faithful have the opportunity to minister to those affected by unexpected pregnancy and abortion, offer to others the peace of Christ
Hail Mary ...

10. May the work of those involved in pro-life movements and abortion recovery inspire our understanding of Scripture that supports life.
Hail Mary ...
Glory Be ...

THE ASCENSION

"Then he led them out as far as Bethany, raised his hands, and blessed them. As he blessed them he parted from them and was taken up to heaven. They did him homage and then returned to Jerusalem with great joy, and they were continually in the temple praising God." (Luke 24:50-53)

Lord, before you ascended into heaven, you gave your disciples supernatural strength through your gift of the Holy Spirit. Filled with joy, confidence, and spiritual power, your followers went to work as your witnesses, to the ends of the earth.

Equip me with that same strength and power, Lord, so I may be a witness for life. Remind me to pray for the lives of the unborn and for couples facing an unexpected pregnancy. Never let me forget to pray for the couple who has experienced an abortion.

Through your Holy Spirit, give me courage to stand outside abortion clinics and plead for the innocent lives of children about to be aborted. Grant me strength to take part in pro-life rallies. Help me to take a stand against legislation that does not protect life from conception to natural death.

Lord, let me be receptive to your call to be a witness for those who cannot speak.

Our Father ...

Petitions:

1. May the mother and father facing an unexpected pregnancy know their child is already destined to belong to the kingdom of God.
Hail Mary ...

2. May the mother and father of the unborn child know the crucified and risen Lord will guide them.
Hail Mary ...

3. May the woman who has had an abortion, and the father of that child, celebrate the promise of the Holy Spirit.
Hail Mary ...

4. May the relatives who have lost a family member through abortion know that Jesus, who has been taken up from the world into heaven, will return in the same way.
Hail Mary ...

5. May the doctors and staff of abortion clinics, and all those who believe that abortion is a woman's right, realize that in an hour they do not expect, the Son of Man will come, and they must be prepared.
Hail Mary ...

6. May the prayer warriors praying on the front lines at abortion clinics and in prayer groups

follow the example of the apostles and devote themselves to prayer.
Hail Mary ...

7. May the Lord bestow his graces on pregnancy help center staff and sidewalk counselors for their dedication to the loving service of God and neighbor.
Hail Mary ...

8. May the priests ministering to those experiencing an unexpected pregnancy and those affected by an abortion send forth the sacred and imperishable proclamation of eternal salvation.
Hail Mary ...

9. May the Church, whose faithful have the opportunity to minister to those affected by unexpected pregnancy and abortion, be Christ's witnesses to the ends of the earth.
Hail Mary ...

10. May those involved in pro-life movements and abortion recovery be a sign for us that God is at work through the people upholding his Word through their prayers and deeds.
Hail Mary ...
Glory Be ...

THE DESCENT OF THE HOLY SPIRIT

"Then there appeared to them tongues as of fire, which parted and came to rest on each one of them. And they were all filled with the Holy Spirit and began to speak in different tongues as the Spirit enabled them to proclaim." (Acts 2:3-4)

Thank you Lord for fulfilling your promise to the apostles by sending the Holy Spirit. Your Word says this promise is also made to me and to my children and to all those far off, whomever you will call.

You have called me, Lord, to wage a battle against abortion. Through your Spirit, you have given me spiritual power. I know this is the same power of the Most High that overshadowed Mary to conceive the Son of God. And it's the same Spirit who raised Jesus from the dead.

Totally armed with this supernatural power from God on high, I am ready to bear witness to the inviolable right to life of every human being. Guide my speech, enlighten my mind, and give me the strength to do your work.

Our Father ...

Petitions:

1. May the Lord show the way to the mother and father facing an unexpected pregnancy.
Hail Mary ...

2. May the mother and father of the unborn child know the promise of the Holy Spirit is made to them and to their children and to all those far off, whomever the Lord our God will call.
Hail Mary ...

3. May the woman who has had an abortion, and the father of that child, meet the comforter, the Spirit of Truth, who Jesus sent to abide with them forever.
Hail Mary ...

4. May the relatives who have lost a family member through abortion realize the Lord's promise that he will not leave us orphans.
Hail Mary ...

5. May the doctors and staff of abortion clinics, and all those who believe that abortion is a woman's right, open their hearts to God to receive the Holy Spirit's extraordinary power of renewal that will change them from the inside out.
Hail Mary ...

6. May the prayer warriors praying on the front lines at abortion clinics and in prayer groups trust in Jesus' promise to work wonders in the heavens above and signs on the earth below.
Hail Mary ...

7. May pregnant couples respond to the Holy Spirit's urging through the pregnancy help center staff and sidewalk counselors and choose life.
Hail Mary ...

8. May the priests ministering to those experiencing an unexpected pregnancy and those affected by an abortion share Jesus' promise that everyone who calls on the name of the Lord shall be saved.
Hail Mary ...

9. May the Church, whose faithful have the opportunity to minister to those affected by unexpected pregnancy and abortion, pour out God's love in a spirit of welcome.
Hail Mary ...

10. May those involved in pro-life movements and abortion recovery spread throughout the world the grace of the Holy Spirit that filled the Upper Room.
Hail Mary ...
Glory Be ...

THE ASSUMPTION

"Finally the Immaculate Virgin, preserved free from stain of original sin, when the course of her earthly life was finished, was taken up body and soul into heavenly glory, and exalted by the Lord as Queen over all things, so that she might be the more fully conformed to her Son, the Lord of lords and conqueror of sin and death."[4]

Catechism of the Catholic Church, 966

Mary, your assumption into heaven is my assurance that I have an intercessor to Jesus. By virtue of your "Yes," God's graces pass through you to me. I know I can accomplish great things through my devotion to you. And you have given us the Rosary for such a time as this. I have faith you will "accompany me, struggle with me, and sustain me in my fight against the forces of evil."[5]

Blessed Virgin Mary, the Mother of all the living, through the prayers of this Rosary, help me to do what is necessary to end abortion and heal all post-abortive families.

Our Father ...

Petitions:

1. May the couple struggling with an unexpected pregnancy know the abiding presence of Mary, who never left the apostles alone.
Hail Mary ...

2. May Mary guide the mother and father of the unborn child to be loving parents.
Hail Mary ...

3. May Mary, the Mother of all the living, who understands the suffering of losing a child, be a refuge to the woman who has had an abortion, and the father of that child.
Hail Mary ...

4. May the relatives who have lost a family member through abortion see the assumption of Mary as their assurance that the faithful will be resurrected.
Hail Mary ...

5. With Mary's help, may the doctors and staff of abortion clinics, and all those who believe that abortion is a woman's right, be rescued from the cruel slavery of the devil.
Hail Mary ...

6. May the prayer warriors praying on the front lines at abortion clinics and in prayer groups be strengthened in their battle against the evil of abortion.
Hail Mary ...

7. May pregnancy help center staff and sidewalk counselors pray for Mary to intercede for pregnant couples so that their spiritual and material needs are met.
Hail Mary ...

8. May the priests ministering to those experiencing an unexpected pregnancy, and those affected by an abortion, turn to Mary to protect and transform their hearts.
Hail Mary ...

9. May the Church, whose faithful have the opportunity to minister to those affected by unexpected pregnancy and abortion, look to Mary as an example of the perfect disciple.
Hail Mary ...

10. May those involved in pro-life movements and abortion recovery reveal to us Mary's Son, Jesus, whose mercy fails no one.
Hail Mary ...
Glory Be ...

THE CORONATION

Mary, Queen of Heaven and Earth, you are the Divine Mother of the King of Kings. God uniquely prepared you to bear his Son by filling you with grace from conception. By your "Yes," you put the plan of salvation into action. Help me respond to God's grace by standing for life.

Satan seeks to wage war against me and anyone who keeps God's commandments. But because of your Son, Jesus, the devil will not prevail. Be my advocate to your Son as I wage the battle for the life of the unborn.

I pray for those who have not decided on which side of the battle they will fight.

Our Father ...

Petitions:

1. May Mary help the mother and father facing an unexpected pregnancy surrender to God's will in all things.
Hail Mary ...

2. May Mary, who gives spiritual birth to all Christians, help the mother and father of the unborn child give birth to their baby.
Hail Mary ...

3. May the woman who has had an abortion, and the father of that child, pray to Mary saying, "If I fall, lead me back to Jesus."
Hail Mary ...

4. May the relatives who have lost a family member through abortion find comfort in the hope that their loved one is in Mary's company.
Hail Mary ...

5. May Mary help the doctors and staff of abortion clinics, and all those who believe that abortion is a woman's right, to be receptive to the action of God.
Hail Mary ...

6. May Mary, the Ark of the New Covenant, help prayer warriors praying on the front lines at abortion clinics and in prayer groups, by speeding their prayers through the gates of heaven.
Hail Mary ...

7. May pregnancy help center staff and sidewalk counselors encourage pregnant couples to trust in the never-failing providence of Jesus, regardless of their circumstances.
Hail Mary ...

8. May Mary nurture with great graces the priests who minister to those experiencing an unexpected pregnancy and those affected by an abortion.
Hail Mary ...

9. May Mary set the hearts of the faithful on fire for Jesus, and give them a burning thirst for souls, so the Church can minister to those affected by unexpected pregnancy and abortion.
Hail Mary ...

10. May those involved in pro-life movements and abortion recovery be an instrument in giving glory to God.
Hail Mary ...
Glory Be ...

APPENDIX

THE PRAYERS OF THE ROSARY

Apostles Creed

I believe in God, the Father Almighty, Creator of heaven and earth; and in Jesus Christ, His only Son Our Lord, who was conceived by the Holy Spirit, born of the Virgin Mary, suffered under Pontius Pilate, was crucified, died, and was buried. He descended into hell; the third day he rose again from the dead; he ascended into heaven, and is seated at the right hand of God, the Father Almighty; from there he shall come to judge the living and the dead. I believe in the Holy Spirit, the Holy Catholic Church, the communion of saints, the forgiveness of sins, the resurrection of the body and life everlasting. Amen.

Our Father

Our Father, who art in heaven, hallowed be thy name; thy kingdom come, thy will be done on earth as it is in heaven. Give us this day our daily bread; and forgive us our trespasses as we forgive those who trespass against us; and lead us not into temptation, but deliver us from evil. Amen.

Hail Mary

Hail Mary, full of grace, the Lord is with thee, blessed art thou amongst women and blessed is the fruit of thy womb, Jesus. Holy Mary, Mother of God, pray for us sinners now and at the hour of our death. Amen.

Glory Be (The Doxology)

Glory be to the Father, the Son, and the Holy Spirit. As it was in the beginning is now and ever shall be, world without end. Amen.

Fatima Prayer #1 (O My Jesus)

O my Jesus, forgive us our sins. Save us from the fires of hell, and lead all souls to heaven, especially, those in most need of your mercy. Amen.

Prayer at the End of Each Decade
(Prayer for Priests)

God, our Father, please send us holy priests, all for the sacred and Eucharistic Heart of Jesus, all for the sorrowful and Immaculate Heart of Mary, in union with St. Joseph. Amen.

Hail, Holy Queen (Salve Regina)

Hail, Holy Queen, Mother of Mercy, our life our sweetness and our hope. To thee do we cry, poor banished children of Eve; to thee do we send up our sighs, mourning and weeping in this valley of tears. Turn then, most gracious advocate, thine eyes of mercy toward us and after this our exile show unto us the blessed fruit of thy womb, Jesus. O clement, O loving, O sweet Virgin Mary!
Pray for us, O Holy Mother of God
That we may be made worthy of the promises of Christ.

Closing Prayer

Let us pray, O God, whose only begotten Son, by his life, death, and resurrection, has purchased for us the rewards of eternal salvation. Grant, we beseech thee, that while meditating on these mysteries of the most Holy Rosary of the Blessed Virgin Mary, that we may imitate what they contain and obtain what they promise, through Christ our Lord. Amen.

Memorare

Remember, O most gracious Virgin Mary that never was it known that anyone who fled to your protection, implored your help, or sought your intercession was left unaided. Inspired with this confidence, we fly to you, O Virgin of virgins, our Mother. To you we come; before you we stand, sinful and sorrowful. O Mother of the Word Incarnate, despise not our petitions, but in your mercy, hear and answer us. Amen.

St. Michael Prayer

St. Michael the Archangel, defend us in battle. Be our protection against the wickedness and snares of the Devil. May God rebuke him, we humbly pray, and do though, O Prince of heavenly hosts, by the power of God, cast into hell Satan, and all evil spirits, who prowl about the world seeking the ruin of souls. Amen.

Fatima Prayer #2 (Most Holy Trinity)

Most Holy Trinity, Father, Son, and Holy Spirit, adore thee profoundly. I offer thee the most precious Body, Blood, Soul and Divinity of Jesus Christ, present in all the tabernacles of the world, in reparation for the outrages, sacrileges and indifference's whereby he is offended. And through the infinite merits of his Most Sacred Heart and the Immaculate Heart of Mary, I beg of thee the conversion of poor sinners.

Fatima Prayer #3

My God, I believe, I adore, I hope, and I love you. I beg pardon of you for those who do not believe, do not adore, do not hope, and do not love you. Mary, Queen of the Holy Rosary, pray for us. Mary, Queen of Peace, pray for us. Mary, Our Loving Mother, pray for us.

THE DAYS OF THE ROSARY

The Catholic Church aligned the mysteries of the Rosary with days of the week to help in praying the Rosary. The days differ slightly during the seasons of Christmas and Lent. This page will help you determine which days the various mysteries of the Rosary are prayed on.

During Ordinary Time:

Sunday – Glorious Mysteries
Monday – Joyful Mysteries
Tuesday – Sorrowful Mysteries
Wednesday – Glorious Mysteries
Thursday – Luminous Mysteries
Friday – Sorrowful Mysteries
Saturday – Joyful Mysteries

During Christmas and Lent:

The difference in praying the Rosary during Christmas and Lent occurs on Sundays. In the Christmas season, the Joyful Mysteries are prayed on Sundays. During the season of Lent, the Sorrowful Mysteries are prayed on Sundays. This shift gives attention to the events in the life of Jesus that are being celebrated during those two seasons—his birth during Christmas and his passion and death during Lent.

Litany of the Blessed Virgin Mary
(Litany of Loreto)

Lord, have mercy	Lord, have mercy
Christ, have mercy	Christ, have mercy
Lord, have mercy	Lord, have mercy
God our Father in heaven	have mercy on us
God the Son,	
Redeemer of the world	have mercy on us
God the Holy Spirit	have mercy on us
Holy Trinity, one God	have mercy on us
Holy Mary	pray for us
Holy Mother of God	pray for us
Most honored of virgins	pray for us
Mother of Christ	pray for us
Mother of the Church	pray for us
Mother of divine grace	pray for us
Mother most pure	pray for us
Mother of chaste love	pray for us
Mother and Virgin	pray for us
Sinless Mother	pray for us
Dearest of mothers	pray for us
Model of motherhood	pray for us
Mother of Good Counsel	pray for us
Mother of our Creator	pray for us
Mother of our Savior	pray for us
Virgin most wise	pray for us

Virgin rightly praised	pray for us
Virgin rightly renowned	pray for us
Virgin most powerful	pray for us
Virgin gentle in mercy	pray for us
Faithful Virgin	pray for us
Mirror of justice	pray for us
Throne of Wisdom	pray for us
Cause of our joy	pray for us
Shrine of the Spirit	pray for us
Glory of Israel	pray for us
Vessel of selfless devotion	pray for us
Mystical Rose	pray for us
Tower of David	pray for us
Tower of ivory	pray for us
House of gold	pray for us
Ark of the Covenant	pray for us
Gate of heaven	pray for us
Morning Star	pray for us
Health of the sick	pray for us
Refuge of sinners	pray for us
Comfort of the troubled	pray for us
Help of Christians	pray for us
Queen of angels	pray for us
Queen of patriarchs and prophets	pray for us
Queen of apostles and martyrs	pray for us
Queen of confessors and virgins	pray for us

Queen of all saints	pray for us
Queen conceived without sin	pray for us
Queen assumed into heaven	pray for us
Queen of the Rosary	pray for us
Queen of families	pray for us
Queen of peace	pray for us
Lamb of God, you take away the sins of the world	have mercy on us
Lamb of God, you take away the sins of the world	have mercy on us
Lamb of God, you take away the sins of the world	have mercy on us
Pray for us, O holy Mother of God,	that we may be made worthy of the promises of Christ.

Let us pray. Eternal God, let your people enjoy content health in mind and body. Through the intercession of the Virgin Mary, free us from the sorrows of this life and lead us to happiness in the life to come. Grant this through Christ our Lord. Amen.

THE 15 PROMISES TO THOSE
WHO RECITE THE ROSARY

The Blessed Virgin Mary promised to Saint Dominic and to all who follow that "Whatever you ask in the Rosary will be granted." She left, for all Christians, 15 promises to those who recite the Holy Rosary.[7]

1. Whoever shall faithfully serve me by the recitation of the Rosary, shall receive powerful graces.

2. I promise my special protection and the greatest graces to all those who shall recite the Rosary.

3. The Rosary shall be a powerful armor against hell; it will destroy vice, decrease sin, and defeat heresies.

4. The Rosary will cause virtue and good works to flourish; it will obtain for souls the abundant mercy of God; it will withdraw the hearts of men from the love of the world and its vanities, and will lift them to the desire for eternal things. Oh, that souls would sanctify themselves by this means!

5. The soul which recommends itself to me by the recitation of the Rosary shall not perish.

6. Whoever shall recite the Rosary devoutly, applying himself to the consideration of its sacred mysteries, shall never be conquered by misfortune. God will not chastise him in his justice, he shall not perish by an unprovided death; if he be just, he shall remain in the grace of God, and become worthy of eternal life.

7. Whoever shall have a true devotion for the Rosary shall not die without the sacraments of the Church.

8. Those who are faithful to recite the Rosary shall have during their life and at their death the light of God and the plentitude of His graces; at the moment of death they shall participate in the merits of the saints in paradise.

9. I shall deliver from Purgatory those who have been devoted to the Rosary.

10. The faithful children of the Rosary shall merit a high degree of glory in heaven.

11. You shall obtain all you ask of me by the recitation of the Rosary.

12. All those who propagate the Holy Rosary shall be aided by me in their necessities.

13. I have obtained from my Divine Son that all the advocates of the Rosary shall have for intercessors the entire celestial court during their life and at the hour of death.

14. All who recite the Rosary are my sons and daughters, and brothers and sisters of my only Son, Jesus Christ.

15. Devotion of my Rosary is a great sign of predestination.

Endnotes:

1. "Map of U.S. Abortion Laws pre-1973." Wikimedia Commons. commons.wikimedia.org. 10 May 2014. Accessed 4 Oct. 2016. URL

2. John Paul II, Evangelium Vitae, Encyclical Letter of His Holiness John Paul II on the Value and Inviolability of Human Life (Washington, D.C.: United States Catholic Conference, 1995), 99

3. Francis, Homily, March 29, 2013, "Way of the Cross at the Colosseum," "Praying the Rosary with Pope Francis," Libreria Editrice Vaticana, (Washington DC: United States Conference of Catholic Bishops, 2014), 43

4. Catechism of the Catholic Church, 2nd ed., Liberia Editrice Vaticana, (Washington DC: United States Catholic Conference, 1997), 966

5. Francis, Homily, August 15, 2013, "Praying the Rosary with Pope Francis," Libreria Editrice Vaticana, (Washington DC: United States Conference of Catholic Bishops, 2014), 51

6. Pius XII, Ad Caeli Reginam On Proclaiming the Queenship of Mary Liberia Editrice Vaticana, (Washington DC: United States Catholic Conference, 11 Oct. 1954), 1

7. Promises given by Our Lady to Blessed Alan de la Roche a Dominican father and promoter of the Rosary (1428-1475), "Praying the Rosary with Pope Francis," Libreria Editrice Vaticana, (Washington DC: United States Conference of Catholic Bishops, 2014), 59

Rosary Meditations from Caritas Press

A MOTHER'S BOUQUET: ROSARY MEDITATIONS FOR MOMS

Straight from the heart of a mother, these rosary meditations for moms will uplift and sanctify your journey. Sherry Boas, author of the critically acclaimed Lily Trilogy, offers these prayers in hopes that moms will grow in holiness and come to more fully treasure the wondrous vocation of motherhood enfolded in the mysteries of Christ's life, death and resurrection. **By Sherry Boas** AVAILABLE IN FULL-COLOR GIFT EDITION AND IN SPANISH

A FATHER'S HEART: ROSARY MEDITATIONS FOR DADS

Discover the heart of true fatherhood as it relates to the life, death and resurrection of Christ. With pearls of wisdom and glimpses into the eternal and relentless love of God, Father Doug Lorig draws on his own experiences as a father and pastor to bring parents to a deeper understanding of their role in God's perfect plan of salvation. Grow in holiness within the wondrous vocation of fatherhood as you pray these rosary written especially for dads. **By Father Doug Lorig**

GENERATIONS OF LOVE: ROSARY MEDITATIONS FOR GRANDPARENTS

Get a glimpse into the heavenly realities of grandparenthood as you come to understand the beautiful and invaluable role you play as parents of parents. Through these insightful and uplifting meditations, Author Anne Belle-Oudry reminds us that, while grandchildren are undoubtedly among life's richest rewards, grandparents, too, are an inestimable blessing to their families as they strive to lead their loved ones closer to Christ through their prayers, example and unconditional love. **By Anne Belle-Oudry**

A CHILD'S TREASURE: ROSARY MEDITATIONS FOR CHILDREN

Grow to love the Lord more deeply through these meditations written by children for children. With insight into how Mother Mary loves Jesus, authors Derek Rebello, Elsa Schiavone and Michael Boas show us how to follow Him more closely in our everyday lives and discover that our faith is truly our greatest treasure. **By Derek Rebello, Elsa Schiavone and Michael Boas**

AMAZING LOVE: ROSARY MEDITATIONS FOR TEENS

Grow to understand the unsurpassed importance of your friendship with Jesus through these rosary meditations written by teens for teens. Authors Mari Seaberg, Adrian Inclan and Maria Boas show how the passion, death and resurrection of Christ sustain our lives today as we strive to do His will in the face of a multitude of decisions, illuminated by his amazing love. **By Adrian Inclan, Mari Seaberg and Maria Boas**

A SERVANT'S HEART: ROSARY MEDITATIONS FOR ALTAR SERVERS

Prepare your heart for true service with these Meditations written especially for altar servers. Reflect on the meaning of your calling as it relates to the mysteries of Christ's life, death and resurrection and as it applies to your own life in a world that is often at odds with the message of Christ's self-sacrificing love. **By Peter Troiano**

Children's Titles from Caritas Press

God's Easter Gifts

Bella and Pablo love Easter egg hunts. So many wonderful goodies just waiting to be found inside each egg! But the brother and sister are about to discover there's much more to Easter than candy and toys, as they embark on a very special Easter egg hunt that will reveal all of God's greatest gifts to us.

Coming Christmas 2017

Bella and Pablo's Christmas Tree

Jackie's Special Halloween

Sister and brother duo Bella and Pablo return in this delightful story about the true meaning of Halloween. Author Brenda Castro captures young imaginations and shows them the truth and beauty of the Faith, just as she does in her acclaimed debut work, God's Easter Gifts.

St. John Bosco & His Big Gray Dog

It is hard to believe that anyone would have ever wanted to hurt good Father John Bosco. He helped so many people. But there were times when his life was in danger. During those times, a very special canine guardian would appear to protect him. In this way, God saved the holy priest from harm so he could complete his mission and help children come to know God.

Encyclopedia of Peg Saints

Discover all the fascinating facts that make the saints so lovable and inspirational. Get to know 36 saints in an engaging and easy to "absorb" format, centered around colorful hand-painted peg dolls collected and cherished by Catholic kids everywhere.

Miraculous Me

What thoughts crossed your mother's mind the first time she laid eyes on you? What dreams did your father hold in his heart? This delightful story by Ruth Pendergast Sissel is told from the perspective of a baby in the womb, listening to his parents' awe at seeing him on ultrasound for the first time.

Barnyard Bliss

The animals can't wait to share the news, Something exciting and beautiful has come to be! A new baby enters the world! All of creation rejoices as word of Mr. And Mrs. Hoot's owlet spreads throughout the farm.

Prolife Books!

With unbridled joy, their voices rise. All things old, become refreshed Welcome Babe! A joyous day! We pray your life be blessed!

Visit CaritasPress.org
(602)920-2846

Amazing Saints & their Awesome Animals Book and Coloring Book

Heart warming stories of sixteen saints and their animal friends. The perfect book for animal lovers.

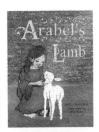

Arabel's Lamb

A young girl's compassion is tested to the limits in this gripping tale about love and sacrifice. Loosely based on the legend of St. George and the Dragon.

Victoria's Sparrows

A young girl, concerned for the welfare of her sparrow friends, discovers God is full of sweet surprises. In classic Sherry Boas style, this brightly illustrated story draws children into the beauty of God's providence and his loving care for all creatures, especially us!

Archangela's Horse

Sometimes God has the most unpredictable ways of showing us the path we are to travel. Archangela comes to understand God's will when her beloved and loyal horse refuses to take her where she wants to go, taking her instead on a joyful journey she never could have imagined.

Gift in the Manger

When their feeding trough ends up serving as a bed for a tiny baby, the animals get a glimpse into God's loving plan to save the world. In this charming fable by seasoned storyteller Sherry Boas, the animals in the stable get a chance to see all the gifts Jesus has brought into the world, all revealed in the tiny baby's eyes.

Little Maximus Myers

never liked being little, until one day, while carrying the cross in the procession at Mass, he discovered how our weaknesses can bring us closer to Christ. Inspired by real-life events of her own children, acclaimed author Sherry Boas weaves a story that will delight and inspire not only altar servers, but all who wish to give their best to Christ despite their own limitations.

Billowtail

Little creatures embark on big adventures on the Way of St. James in Medieval Spain.

Visit CaritasPress.org
(602)920-2846

Caritas Press was founded in 2011 with the mission of shedding light on things eternal in a culture that is becoming increasingly blind to the wonders of God's works and numb to His boundless love. Making use of the subtle and the beautiful, Caritas Press hopes to play a part in igniting in children and adults a desire to know God more fully. For a full listing of all Caritas titles for children, youths and adults, visit CaritasPress.org.

Fiction from Caritas Press

Until Lily
Wherever Lily Goes
Life Entwined with Lily's
The Things Lily Knew
Things Unknown to Lily
A Little Like Lily

"...You will be entranced, you will experience the joys and sorrows of the characters, you will cry, and you will not be able to put Lily down."
– Dr. Jeff Mirus of CatholicCulture.org

The transforming power of love is at the heart of this poignant series about the people whose lives are moved by a woman with Down syndrome. Lily's story is told with such brutal yet touching honesty, it will have you laughing one minute and reduced to tears the next.

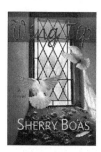

Wing Tip

Dante De Luz's steel was forged in his youth, in the crucible of harsh losses and triumphant love. But that steel gets tested like never before as his mother's deathbed confession reveals something startling about his father and presents the young Catholic priest with the toughest challenge of his life, with stakes that couldn't get any higher.

"Sure to be a Catholic Classic"
"Magnificent read"
Robert Curtis, Catholic Sun

Made in the USA
Columbia, SC
01 July 2020

13072949R00055